CW00507446

T

Changing

Temperatures

of

Heartache

Cassie Senn

C.H.S

Copyright

The Changing Temperatures of Heartache
Copyright © 2020 Cassie Senn
All rights Reserved
No part of this book may be used or reproduced in any
context without written and documented permission, except
in the context of reviews.

Instagram: @poems.c.h.s

For those who know me personally, please do not be
alarmed by my words. I share not solely my own stories, but
also those of others I know, have seen or hear about.

Hillel circa 50 BC
"If I am not for myself, who will be for me? And if I am for
myself alone, what am I? And if not now, when?"

For Mum
For N.I.C.K.
For all the family, blood or not
For current friends
For past friends, and future ones
For crushes, old and new
For my soul mate, wherever you are
For you

This book isn't a lot of things.

It's not going to tell you how you should feel. It's not going to be able to solve your problems or tell you what to do. It's not going to be able to cure your heartache, stop the pain or make someone love you. It's just not; but that's ok.

This book full of poems, I guess if you can call them poems, this book full of words and all the god damn emotions you could ever feel isn't meant to do any of those things, and to be fair I don't think any object could. This book I have written and put together is simply here in the hope that some of you might be able to relate to a few of the situations, some of the feelings.

This book is a reminder that you aren't alone, even if you really feel like it someone, somewhere, is probably experiencing the same thing. Reading this won't solve anything but I have the hope it might ease the burdens on your heart and mind slightly, even if only by an inch, because for me just by writing the thoughts and emotions that have flown through my head, down on these pages, it's certainly helped.

So, this book is for you, all of you.

All of you people out there who are falling in love, are in love, have been loved, have loved others so damn much, who have been hurt, who are still hurt.

Those who are confused, who question who they are, who don't know their real identity, who have a family, have no family, are missing key members of that family, who want a family, who are creating their own, for those who don't know where they belong, who don't have a real home, who are making a home.

For those who have been punched in more ways than one, physically, mentally, for those who have been violated and those who haven't and god I hope you never will, those who are happy, those who are not, for those who are alone or even very much together and for everyone else in this fucked up, messed up, but god damn beautiful world.

This is for you.

I. Raw

The wounds, old and new, they are still raw.

It's sad how you can feel yourself drifting away from your best friend and no matter how far you extend your arm they make no effort to reach out.

(I miss spending time with you)

Honestly, I just fucking miss you, I miss the people we used to be. The carefree, happy children that we were, in families which seemed perfect and untouchable. We had our own little worlds, our own connection with none of this bullshit drama or worries. Oh, what I would do to go back to those moments, even for a single minute; where you and me were indestructible, the two best friends against the world.

(Even though we have grown apart you mean the world to me, please don't forget that.)

I've changed. I'm not the same person I used to be,
All those years ago when I was smaller and carefree.

One of the hardest things is looking at someone you have known all your life and realising you no longer really know them.

Sometimes I wished we'd stayed in touch, I cared about you a lot back then and even now I still do. I hope you're okay.

(Wishes from a distant friend)

Friendship is a strange thing, looking back so many people in that part of your life were so important to you, but now all you have are the memories and ghosts of them.

It's a frightening thing that someone who you can be so unbelievably close with, the person who knows your secrets, your hopes, your dreams, that in the matter of a few months they can become simply a stranger and nothing more.

We are are barely more than strangers. There is no real acknowledgement when we pass and it's funny because we went through a lot together and I trusted you with so much of myself. Now we hardly know each other, which shouldn't be the case because of our history, but it is. We have both changed, I don't recognise the person you are now, and I think maybe that was always what was meant to happen. We needed each other, for a year, to become the people we were meant to be and find those we were meant to be with.

People are so much like tourists, fleeting, they will stay in your life for a short while and then get on a plane and disappear never to be seen again, gone. You just need to find the ones who never want to leave.

And that's just how life goes, maybe some people are only meant to be an important part of your life for a small amount of time, and others forever.

I wonder how many memories I have been a part of, and how many of those have been forgotten.

If someone doesn't want to be in your life you can't force them; and at the end of the day, it's them that's missing out.

When the first man you see, the one who should love you unconditionally fails you, how can you expect others to be any different?

He left me so why should I trust you, when you say you won't?

I search everywhere for memories of a man I have never met. Forgotten whispers, smiles, a twinkle of eyes that have never reached mine. Faded photographs, yellowed with age, that show a different man; a distant relative, a stranger, but one that I would have liked you to have been. One that there were traces of having breathed and lived.

Evidence that somewhere maybe you do exist.

Nearly all the men in my life have been fleeting, although maybe boys are more appropriate than men. They reeked of cowardice, of lies, of deceit. They ran, they ghosted, or just gently faded when they either got what they wanted, didn't get it or couldn't handle the truth. God, the truth, the truth is what they are all afraid of, they can't own up or take responsibility for their own actions and decisions and that's what makes them boys rather than men. Truth.

Do you feel guilty?
Do you feel regret?
Do you ever wonder about me?
What I look like, what I've become, if I'm at all like you?
Do you ever wish you had done things differently?
Do you ever think about what could have been?
Do you wish you'd never disappeared to live your perfectly
planned life which didn't include me?
Have you ever thought about contacting me?
Have you ever looked?
Have you ever tried?

Did you ever love me?

(Questions for a father who left and never looked back.)

A part of me might want you but I don't need you. I have never needed you these past 18 years. My mum has been more than enough; better than any mum I could have hoped for and better than you could have ever been. My mum has been my rock, the anchor holding me down, and the scaffolding keeping me up. I owe her everything and I owe you nothing.

(Extract from Dear Dad)

II. Melting

I'm still unsure about this crush
Whether it will melt my heart, or if it will remain cold.

And I can feel it happening again, the strange middle ground between liking you that way and just being friends. I know it's gonna fuck me over, I can tell, I just wish I knew how this was going to end.

Mixed signals

It's the x's at the end of the message,
It's the brush of an arm, a leg, a hand
It's the silent sideways looks and the lean when you speak
those soft words.
But it's also another girl you mention,
Someone else you drink for and not me.
It's the lack of embrace at the end of a night, walking away,
no proper goodbye,
But only sometimes,
Some days it's there, the hug, the pause, unwillingness to let
go and to move on
You give me that look, and I feel something, a connection
But one that only half belongs to me, if even at all.
Maybe it's just another of these mixed signals.

If there is ever someone I think about the most, it's you. You're the one person who's left more of an impact on me than anyone without even realising. You are completely and utterly ingrained into my mind and no matter what I do you're. I have spent so many sleepless nights analysing all the slight glances and half smiles you throw my way and questioning how I can feel so much for someone I hardly even know.

(You are the one thought that repeats itself over and over in my head)

And suddenly I'm hit with the sinking feeling, that all of this is just wishful thinking

Someone asked me if I was catching feelings for you again. The thing is I don't think they ever left.

This crush on you is so compressing and suffocating because I know nothing will ever happen because you have found the one you love, but I can't help these feelings from erupting no matter how hard I try and suppress them. And god I know we are just friends maybe not even that maybe just acquaintances, but the fact that every time you see me you smile and wave and will make an effort to say hi or comment on my new hair really isn't helping me from moving on and god it just ends up crushing me more.

I am falling in love with you, and its heart-breaking and devastating, utterly soul destroying because I have never had this feeling for anyone before and maybe not for anyone else again and yet this could all be for nothing. All this feeling and whirlwind of emotion may just result in silence and empty space because they are simply not returned and instead, you're in love with someone else.

I shouldn't be jealous because you were never even mine

Ever since the first day my gaze fell upon you, I've been falling; slowly but surely, every goddamn day I've been falling for you. Deeper, deeper, and deeper still, and I know I shouldn't, you're just so unobtainable, so far out of my reach no matter how far I stretch towards you there's never going to be a point where you look at me any differently; and god that kills me inside.

(You're blissfully unaware of me and god I wish I was blissfully unaware of these feelings I have for you)

The more time I spend with you the harder this gets, because darling my feelings are growing by the day, by the second and I need to know if this is something which will end before its even begun or if there is something between us. That you feel something too.

I look into your eyes, and even after so long apart the feelings still arise, and I'm surprised you can't tell because it seems as if my feelings for you are pouring out of every pore, they roll off my tongue in silent words which surely you should have heard. They crackle with electricity every time we touch, when our arms brush and yet you still don't have a clue. God if only you knew.

And so now we're talking, but I don't know if it's as friends or something more, and I'm trying not to reply too quickly, or leave your messages for too long. Sometimes there are x's, sometimes not, and your use of emojis, or lack of, says a lot. You're active, but don't read them, or straight away you click and view. But either way, anything you do, it makes my stomach flutter and despite all the mixed signals you've melted my heart as easily as butter.

Maybe crushes aren't such a bad thing after all.

Underneath all this longing, the chaos of wanting to be the one you hold and the heartache, that long dull ache when things don't work out the way you had always hoped, there is a beauty. These feelings have a beauty about them, and their sheer honesty and desire reminds us of our capability to love and trust within each other. And what could be better than small reminders of all this love you can and will give out into this world.

I will always be grateful for these moments we have, when such small encounters create such huge waves in my being, and feelings, oh the feelings!

You are the type of person I simply want in my life, as a lover or as a friend, but I would love for us to be more than just a smile and a wave.

And maybe that's what we forget about crushes, that they set the foundations of what could become.

From the moment that we caught eyes across the room there was this strange connection, and it has grown ever since. Every message, every laugh, it all contributes to this feeling between us and whether it's simply as friends, or lovers, or a strange middle ground between the two, I don't really mind because you're in my life and right now that's all that matters.

(I know the exact moment our souls found each other, and I hope they never let go)

These butterflies I feel and the giddiness when you walk past
is perhaps just the beginning,
Perhaps this will turn into something more.

You have a smile that could melt even the coldest of hearts honey.

III. Hot

Your hands brush delicately across my skin, I bite my lip and try to conceal the hot pink which has flushed upon my cheeks.

You've got my stomach doing flips, circus tricks.

Our hands brush together, fingertips tingling, beaming smiles on our faces that we are so desperately trying to conceal because the temperature is rising between us and we both want to keep this heat alive for as long as we can.

Knees pressed together, shoulders gently touching, the brush of an arm, god my skin has never felt so alive.

The way you look at me, it makes my heart flutter
Over and over again, my worries simply
Melt, and I just want to be yours.

We were laying in my bed for the first time, your arms wrapped around me and our silence like this blanket of warmth draped over our bodies making me feel safer than ever before.

You asked me what my guilty pleasure was
and I didn't have a clue,
But I've finally figured it out.
It's you. It was always you.

Our first kiss made all the others seem like tiny specks of dust, and this, well this was an entire storm.

Trace my features with your fingers, those very fingers which turn those velvet pages when we are sat in our favourite coffee shop, losing ourselves to other worlds and absorbing delicate words. Those fingers that knit themselves with mine, pulling me through the grass to the swings where the children in our hearts belong and we believe we have wings. Brush my skin softly, use those fingers that I love to tie me in knots, and then undo me. If only you knew I'm at mercy to your fingers, you and only you.

It's those random messages that make me giggle and the quiet smile at just the thought of you that really makes me believe in this, in us.

I can see the sparkle in your eyes when you talk about your family; those bright blue orbs glimmering. I'm getting so lost in them.

I can smell the scent of you almost everywhere, especially on your hoodies I took. I don't think I'll ever give them back.

I can hear your heart pounding in your chest and your deep breaths in this silent room. I could listen to you all night.

I can feel the ridges of your ribcage through your shirt and the rough but loved skin on your palms. I never want to let go.

I can taste strawberries, mint and love on your lips. I never thought I'd adore those flavours as much as I do.

(All five of my senses are telling me I'm in love with you.)

Falling in love with you was one of the easiest things to do.

And we are sat there, fingers intertwined, and I just can't believe you're mine.

We are sat on the very sofa where all those months ago I caught your eye, and you smiled while crossing the room. Your head is in my lap, hands intertwined like on our first date when you pulled me along the boardwalk under the red lights; us throwing our heads back and laughing like the children we are inside our souls. I can sense you tracing my features with your gaze and honestly, I have never felt so much warmth, so I looked down and I said I love you!

We were lying in my bed, 10am on a Thursday morning wishing we could stay like that forever. Your fingers on my inner wrist, swollen lips and the thud of heartbeats. Everything felt right, finally the pieces fit together and the puzzles of our hearts were complete. I didn't think it could get any better until you whispered those soft words to me, and I looked into your bright brown eyes and knew you truly meant them.

(I love you...)

(I love you too…)

I couldn't be happier if I'm honest, your hands are round my waist, your breath against my neck and my heart is well and truly yours.

(It couldn't be in better hands)

It's all those little secret moments that I crave. The sneaky kiss outside of the pub doors before anyone sees us, wandering hands underneath tables and the gentle caress on our wrists. It's all the jokes that only the two of us understand, comments lost on those around us who don't get the context and I like it that way, along with those cheeky squeezes, not only in the bedroom but also random risky places, like train stations and in front of our friends. But honestly, I wouldn't have it any other way.

Because of you I realised that I am capable of loving with my whole heart, with every inch of my body, every pore. I've learned that I can be loved fully and that I can love fully; that's because of you.

And I wasn't really looking for you, you just waltzed into my life with that smirk on your lips and bright brown eyes that have specks of orange when the sun hits them. And soft hands and an even softer laugh that warmed my insides the instant I heard it ring through my ears. Your pure and beautiful soul is the stuff people dream of, but what I never looked for because I thought it would be impossible to find until you found me. Oh, what a case of serendipity.

I look at you softly, your eyes calm, hidden under dense lashes and in my head I list everything I love about you, all the big things and all the small things, like how I know when you want to kiss me by the way your eyes flicker and how sometimes you twitch in your sleep, and the noise you make first thing in the morning when you stretch all ready for the day ahead; and I always lose track of what I've said to myself because you are full of so much beauty and your soul is so marvellous that I don't think there's a single thing I couldn't love about you.

I'm not used to so much happiness, but I want to be. I want these quiet nights in with you to last forever, for you to look at me and only me like that, with a small smirk on your lips and sparkly eyes. I treasure these walks we have, the confidence in your stride and the giggle that is always rising in me along with those fluttery butterflies trapped in my stomach, and the moments when we sneak a kiss in a crowd full of strangers rushing by, and it's as if time has stopped; when your lips brush mine, and God there is nothing more divine. I never want to lose you because trust me I don't think I could be much happier than this.

I could say the words ten thousand times a day, shower you in soft kisses and constantly interlace my fingers with yours but I don't think any of this would truly express my feelings for you.

(They are nameless, they are indescribable, they are beyond anything and everything)

Sometimes I think I say the words too much, that maybe they are becoming repetitive, a habit, but every time they leave my mouth, I remember just how honest they are. You are one of the best things to have happened to me and I constantly want to remind you of that. You have made me the happiest I have been for a long time and the words couldn't be more true, I love you, I really do.

I wish you could see what I see when I look at you. One of the most stunning, kind-hearted and genuine souls stands before me and you just don't seem to realise how incredible you are. There is beauty in everything that you do, from the way you stretch, or run your hands through your hair in the morning when you've just woken up. You never fail to make me laugh or smile and your consideration for others is second to none. Your personality matches your gorgeous exterior, and I just simply adore you inside and out.

(I love you, I love you, I love you)

As every day goes by, I seem to fall in love with you more and more.

Being with you is blissful, it's that feeling of lying in a flowering meadow, freckles in full bloom, sun dancing over skin, painting it in light and colour and hearts full of such awe at all the good things in the world. All the pure things, and all the true things such as you.

I love you, and gosh do I miss every little thing about you. Your smell, the way your hair is all messy in the mornings and the way you wake up and pull me close into your chest. I miss the light in your eyes when you get all the answers right in a quiz and the way you look at me full of love. There is not a day that goes by when I don't think about you and wish I was snuggled up with my head on your shoulder, fingers laced together squeezing your hand, but I guess this will have to do. I love you.

(Long distance lovers)

and as the sun slips down behind the clouds and buildings, dips past the horizon, the sky is tinged with the same pink that rises up on my cheeks when you throw a wonky grin my way; I know another day has gone by where I've had the pleasure of being in love with you.

(Your beauty reminds me of sunsets and so much more)

All the past heartbreak, all the pain, all the upset was worth it because without all of it I wouldn't have been led to you. I wouldn't spend my evenings laughing with the man I love or have lazy mornings lying with our hearts pressed together. I am thankful for the past for making me the person I am today, the one who is madly in love with you and truly, truly happy.

IV. Burning

Sometimes the water ends up too hot
And someone ends up getting burned.

The flames always licked at our toes no matter how hard we tried to push them away

The tension between us is thick and heavy, almost suffocating. The red wine on the floor has not only stained and tainted the carpet underneath our very feet but our relationship too. The broken glass ready like our tongues to inflict wounds at any second and I am scared to breathe because any movement could shake the foundations of our togetherness and we have already been through too many earthquakes to sustain any more damage. We are held together by mere threads; we are one spark away from igniting everything into flames and finally destroying what burnt away a long time ago but what denial tried to piece back together.

(Our love burnt away a long time ago, we were just too darn scared to admit it.)

Here's the thing, you never opened up to me so how was I ever meant to know you were burning and needed me to extinguish the flames.

I cared for you, I really did and god I wanted this to work, but you lit your matches and burned the bridge between us at the first opportunity that you got and those flames roared at our heels and destroyed any chances of fixing this mess that you created. And as I desperately tried to drench the flames you just stood there, stood there and watched like you didn't care and god maybe you never did.

A recipe for disaster.
Have two people,
Add in a burning desire.
Place them by a worn-out fire.
Give one a cup full of lust;
The other brimming with mistrust.
Let them drink, swallow it all.
Let the sun set and night fall.
Wait. Watch. Listen. See.
A disaster will form. It's a guarantee.

And in a matter of minutes all of my confidence that was built around me has been shattered, like a glass house all my panes, and walls, and roof; all my security has been destroyed.

Your relationship is still toxic if they constantly push you down in order for them to appear higher than you. Or if they leave once, twice, three times, or even ten; breaking your heart and then returning in order to simply do the same thing again. He's toxic if his words shake you right down to the foundations of who you are, shattering like an earthquake, your soul and mind and she's toxic if she enjoys taunting and messing with your head like a board game where the ladders are all broken and the snakes are out to get you.

(Toxic isn't necessarily physical abuse; it's not always fists and punches.)

Shattered glass on our bedroom floor, as if my heart wasn't enough and you just had to break more.

No matter how many times I try to rewrite the script it always ends this way, a terrible tragedy.

THOSE VERY HANDS WHICH USED TO CUP MY
FACE AND THREAD THEMSELVES THROUGH MY
HAIR GENTLY EVERY NIGHT WHEN MY HEAD
WAS IN YOUR LAP ARE NOW THE ONES WHICH
CAUSE ME TO BE BLACK AND BLUE AS EASILY AS
A PEACH, AND CAUSE THE PAIN THAT I KNOW
YOU CAN SEE REFLECTED IN MY EYES AND YET
YOU DON'T CARE DO YOU?

The blackness and blueness I feel on the inside, now thanks to you, it's visible on the outside.

There's a poison that runs through your veins, but I only realised once it had seeped into me too.

I don't know how on earth we came to this. You are screaming darts of poison right into me while I'm staring at my shaking hands trying to apologize for something I should not have to be sorry for, while watching the man I fell in love with become exactly like all the others even when you said you weren't like them, and you promised. You promised me that, but now I'm weeping and begging for forgiveness as if I'm the enemy, the one who declared war and you are just a mere victim, even when you promised this wouldn't happen, that this was in the past with all the other men, the other manipulators, who make it out to be our fault when it's not. They switch the roles and somehow they are the vulnerable ones, who I should be apologising to, even though it's me, me, me I AM THE VICTIM OF YOU

(You promised you weren't like them but after time, it all ends the same)

I hate you.

I hate you for making me feel so worthless and weak, like I was the one who was undeserving and had a cruel heart. That all of my past mistakes and decisions had led me to this and how undeserving I was of anything more, anything better than your hands on me, on my cheeks, on my wrists gripping hard and a shove against the wall. Your breath in my ear whispering small bullets that flow into my brain and become lodged there, small land mines of uncertainty, doubt and self-hatred that could explode at any moment, completely uprooting me and destroying any last strands of stability and hope.

I hate myself most of all.

I hate myself for not seeing your toxicity sooner, not trusting my gut and walking away when I wasn't sure it felt right. I kick myself every night for not escaping sooner and now not being strong enough to trust myself and get the hell out of here because maybe now I'm reliant on you and maybe now I do somewhat believe that this is what I deserve and that I am not worth anything better but god I hate myself for having these thoughts even run across my mind because it's you.

It's you that's full of venom.

You are the undeserving one.

You are the one that should hate yourself, for what you've become.

Boys like you

It's boys like you, you are the ones that make us feel like shit, that lie, that disrespect. All you spouted from those lips of yours were lies and poison. You said what you thought I wanted to hear, not that you meant any of that shit. The manipulation in those words was so god damn strong, if only I had realised it sooner, how you were only here for one thing; for your own wants and petty needs. And when you didn't get it, even after all the lies and the guilt you tried to push upon me, I was suddenly a tease. I was frigid, I wasn't giving it up, hell I wasn't because I didn't want to and you should never question the choices about my body I make or make me justify why because it's not for you to decide. It never has been and it sure as hell never will be.

I do not need to justify or explain myself to you,
I never will, and I never should.
So, don't you dare try and pressure any words from my lips,
When the only one that is of any importance is NO.

And to this day you don't think anything was wrong that night, it is like you were almost in a different room because I don't understand how you can't have picked up on how I felt, and I don't understand how even now looking back you dismiss my feelings with a snap of your fingers. Maybe you didn't mean for me to feel the way I did, but you can't push aside my emotions simply because it's easier for you, because it's convenient, because it's less effort than trying to listen and comprehend.

(You have no right to tell me how I should or shouldn't have felt, no right at all)

No is a stop sign
A red light
A no entry road.
You respect it.
Do not disregard it

You fucking hurt me, the way you acted and treated me was disgusting and I don't understand how you can have that little respect for me, the girl you were supposedly falling for, or for any woman to even begin with.

I wanted this to go well, I wanted us to be something at least, even if it didn't end up being lovers, I would have loved you as a friend because I did care about you and that's the most tragic part. I actually cared for you, so I would never have wished any of this on you and I still wish there wasn't such a rift and line between us because I never wanted there to be one and it hurts because you were the one to draw it. You did that when you removed yourself from my life so easily as if you had never really been there and as though you had never really cared in the first place, like all of this was some made up dream in my head and there was never even an us.

I believed you'd changed, trusted those words you poured out to me at 3am, tears streaming from your eyes one phrase rolling over and over in your mouth, your tongue reeling it out as quickly as it could,

"This will never happen again, I am so sorry, I swear I've changed."

God wasn't I stupid,

To believe that you actually meant any of that.

I don't hate you, but I hate the way you treated me. Flirting with someone else behind my back god have some fucking decency. A year and 3 months together means surely I deserve more respect, couldn't you have waited till after you broke up with me before you moved on to someone else.

And I don't care if your hands didn't touch her body, your words did. They caressed her soft skin in a way they hadn't touched me, for months.

Distance is supposed to make the heart grow fonder, not wander like yours did.

For once I thought I'd fallen for a decent boy, one with a kind heart to match his soft smile, but of course it was too good to be true.

Why did you change?

V. Numb

You are gone from my side after all these years and now all I can feel is pure emptiness, you have left me numb.

Maybe the hardest part for me is that I struggle to write about it, the right words just don't come out, the page stays blank. I cannot create a poem about you or what you did that is true to my heart and feelings, it's the part of me I just can't express and god I hate you for that.

(I want to spill it all out onto these soft pages and forget it ever even happened.)

Even through all the torment, the harassment, even after all of it stopped it was like you still had this hold on me. I was drawn to you and repulsed at the same time, repulsed at why there was this connection after all the shit you put me through and how uncomfortable and utterly shit I felt every time you opened your mouth. Those words, those comments, those gestures they all got into my head, they messed with my emotions, my heart, and god even now when a picture of you popped up there was that drop of the stomach, the memories, the uneasy feeling which I thought had left a long time ago. I thought I had numbed all the remains of you, but they all came back clear as day.

Everything I see now is just grey.

You've taken all my colour away.

It's these silent nights with empty sheets,
There's only one pair of shoes, for one set of feet.
Why do you refuse to return my calls?
There's never a knock, you're never at the door.
My heartbreak playlist is always on repeat.
Pictures of us, or you, I just can't delete.
I loved you with every part of me, every pore.
So why did you destroy me right down to the core?

Leave if you want, its fine but please, please, give back every breath of mine you ever took. All the silent words muffled by your soft lips. And the 3am phone calls and blinding laughter we shared; because I see you everywhere and it all reminds me of you, and I can't cope having to live remembering the last lingers of your touch or any part of your existence without curling in tear stained sheets with ripped up pillows trying to calm my broken being.

(I'm angry, 'fine' really means I'm breaking)

There are some things you can say only to your bedroom ceiling

I lie here in tear stained sheets crying to the moon and the stars because they are the only ones here to comfort me. Their gentle gleam painting my skin with pale light, softly, they whisper to me through the wind. All the souls have gone to sleep my love, you are safe they say, and as those words touch my skin I break. I break and sink deeper into the bed and stare up to the sky howling to the moon,

Why doesn't he love me like you do?

You are everywhere, fucking everywhere. In every song we danced or fell asleep humming along to, on the long bus journeys from yours to mine. In every book we flicked through on a lazy Thursday and the random notes I still find in my cupboard drawers. I will never drag my fingers through your hair again or murmur into your chest, but you are still here. You are everywhere.

Your perfume stuck on my favourite sweater,
Your eyes glimmering like this autumn weather,
Reminding me of how you treated me better.
Your favourite songs making me remember,
All the memories of when we were together,
Reminding me that I should have treated you better

I'm sat at 4am pouring my heart out onto pages you'll never read.

You'll never read these words on tear stained pages,

Nor will you ever hear my screams at 2am muffled by the pillow where you used to lay your head,

You'll never push back my hair to smell the perfume that I now try to drown myself in with the hope it will reach out to you.

You'll never come back, no matter what I do.

A month later and I'm still writing poems about you, so maybe you leaving had more of an impact on me than I first thought.

(I stand in the rain for reasons strangers may not understand)

I need the rain. I need the smell of it to mask your scent which you left on all my clothes and etched into my skin.

I pray for rain. I pray these drenching droplets will wash away all the memories of you and cleanse my soul from the grief and heartache you caused me.

I beg for rain. I beg the rain to break the chains which bind me to you like ivy, so very tight because I cannot move on from you if any part of my body or being is still held within your grasp.

I need, I pray, I beg for rain.

I just want to feel again, I'm sick and tired of being stuck in this ice, of feeling emotionless and numb because I know it won't bring you back to me, nothing could.

VI. Bitter

THERE IS SO MUCH GOD DAMN BITTERNESS
RUNNING THROUGH MY VEINS BECAUSE OF YOU

No matter how fucking hard I scrub at my skin, till it's numb and bleeding, your fucking fingerprints remain, etched deep into my flesh and I can't get them to leave like the rest of your presence did.

The sour taste in my mouth still won't leave.

Even after you did.

You didn't even tell your friends why things ended, I must have meant that little to you.

Don't go near him
He'll just break your heart
Leave you in tears
With multiple scars

(Lessons I've learnt the hard way)

By now you're going to be at least five girls over us, but I can still taste your lips and feel your breath on my skin.

Now I'm just sat here burning Polaroid pictures of us.
What a waste.

Thousands of days, millions of seconds we spent together, and you repay me with this? I gave every inch of my soul to you knowing you could break me, but you promised you wouldn't. Yet you did; and that promise was destined to crumble the moment it left your lips; but I just couldn't see it. Oh, how I wish I could have. Then maybe my heart would still be in one piece and my breath would not choke me each time your name floats through the air. You ruined us. You ruined me. Completely.

(Maybe if I had never met you, I would be happy now.)

IF YOU TRULY LOVED ME, CARED FOR ME,
VALUED ME LIKE YOU SAID THEN WHY DID YOU
LEAVE ME THE WAY THAT YOU DID?

I should have run from you from the start, but your gaze kept me rooted to the spot. If I had never looked at you, maybe I wouldn't have fallen apart.

(My life is full of things I should or shouldn't have done)

I foolishly place my trust, so easily, in the people I should really be running away from.

(Why do I never learn?)

"You didn't have to fall for me"

What can I do when your gaze keeps me rooted to the ground, unable to flee? What can I do, when those devastatingly deep eyes draw me in and I'm drowning in danger?

You have me hooked and I can't resurface.

What can I do when your touch is the only thing that crosses my mind, and time slows when your breath dusts my skin, what can I do? What can I do when you were the one who made me fall in love with you?

How can there be anything which will help me fall out of love with you; when there was nothing to stop me in the first place, from crumbling at your knees with just the knowledge of your existence?

(If you were happy then why did you leave?)

Three years of love and care became tiring for you. Nothing was wrong, just the rush of excitement had faded into the background. Our love, our life had become a routine, it was the same every day, continuous. But shouldn't that be what love's about? It should be constant, always there, always felt. Maybe she's a challenge or a chase, maybe you get a buzz of freshness and change. But tell me when your love for her ages, loses the blindness of being new, will you be happy then? Or will you wander again searching for happiness, when you've already left it behind.

I'm happy but I could be happier. Those were the most toxic words you could have ever spoken and the way in which you uttered them with no remorse, no emotion made it all the worse and I still don't understand how the switch flipped in your head and all of a sudden I wasn't enough and maybe I was never enough but then why did you lie and say you were happy? Because if you were, if you truly were you wouldn't have done this, but god underneath it all I'm so glad that I'm not with someone who could play pretend for so long until someone better came along. But I'm doubtful if anyone will ever make you happy. With a heart of stone like yours I don't think anyone will be enough for you.

I hope you cringe when you hear my name. That the thought of my presence makes your skin crawl. That your chest tightens with the memories of the past. I hope you are haunted by your actions and that what you did to me still weighs you down with guilt because that is perhaps the only way I can be free.

(I hope to hell you feel some form of regret)

When you run your hands over her body, trace the indents of her figure, the soft lines of her skin, do you ever have thoughts of me? Does your mind cast you back to all those times we were in that exact same position, of the times we spent together, the times we fell asleep in each other's arms, just like you are doing now, right now. Does it feel the same, better even, or does it feel wrong? God I hope it feels wrong, I hope it is my name on your lips that you have to swallow back and that it's my eyes you wish you were drowning in, and that all those memories of me flood your senses reminding you of what you lost. What you're never getting back.

I hope you saw me, god I hope you looked real hard and saw how happy, how great I was doing without you. I hope the sight of me stirred up those old feelings or maybe even better, they never went away but lurched even harder at the sight of me reminding you of what you threw away, what you lost. Damn, I hope I reminded you of what went wrong, where you went wrong, and where you are never going again.

Fuck you, you are never going to read these poems. You are never going to get a glimpse of my precious emotions or deepest thoughts, nor will you ever be exposed to the rawest parts of my soul or depths of my heart and mind because damn. You do not deserve it. No, you don't deserve to read a single word.

VII. Thawing

I've begun to accept it all now, I understand, I can start to move on. The curtain has been opened and the sun has finally been allowed to gently flow into my heart. Spring has begun, the bitterness will thaw.

I forbid you from affecting me anymore, I refuse to let your presence alter me because you aren't worth it. I am done wasting valuable time, thoughts of you circling round in my head when you don't belong there.

I have pushed you out of every pore, you are no longer welcome underneath my skin.

You left me for someone else,

And I wonder if you ever really loved me,

When you were growing feelings for them.

You were only interested in me when there was no one better around.

(It's sad how easily some people can be influenced by others.)

It's a fine line between loving the idea of someone, and actually loving them.

You felt like home to me.
I was charmed, I was at ease.
And maybe that was the problem.
You were home for far too many people.

And maybe my biggest flaw was that I always saw the best in you. Even when there was none to be seen.

That uncertainty, that little nagging voice in the back of your mind, is usually right my dear. Please listen to it sooner, for your own sake.

(Trust your gut, your instincts are key for keeping your heart safe and your mind steady.)

I knew I couldn't have you,
So I wrote down all the features I liked about you,
Then I knew what to look for in someone else.

And sometimes you have to take a step back because as much as you like that one person and as much as your heart leaps for them and only them, sadly they are not for you. And as painful and heart-breaking as it is you have to listen to the truth; you have to let them go because they deserve their own happiness and sometimes it just doesn't lie with you.

I may not be okay now, but I will be.

I know I will.

Like flowers, I will bloom again. I will rise from the dust, little shoots forcing their way through the dirt you buried me under. I will not be dormant forever; I will become stronger and brighter and more colourful than I ever was with you.

Trust me, you'll be jealous of my bloom.

I must let you go in order to free myself, so that is what I'm doing.
Dropping the shackles and spreading my wings.

Farewell can be just as enchanting as hello

It's time, time to let my feelings for you go off into the wind. The air picks up the remains you left in me and carries them back, and as I open up my heart to the sky in order to cleanse you from my soul, I whisper up to the clouds "take care, you are on your own now".

It's funny how one person can suddenly change things for you.

After you I was more cautious, I was scared to open up because of the risk and the only result I knew was pain. Maybe you made me more cynical because I swear I wasn't this distrustful and wary and suspicious before. But you gave me good reason to be, because at the end of the day you were not the type of person that you said you were; so can you really blame me? You ruined places, and songs and smells. It took at least 5 more trips to the place of our last date for it to longer hold any ties to you, the bad memories were replaced with much better ones, it just took me time. But still to this day your smell haunts me and I know straight away when you're near because it's the one thing I can't erase from my mind, still after all this god damn time.

I do have to thank you though, in some ways you changed me for the better. You made me realise my worth and how I deserved so much better than you ever treated me, or how you ever acted around me. I know what to not settle for, and trust me I won't be making the same mistake again. You taught me to trust my gut, follow my instincts because god they were right, so awfully right. I knew something was wrong, something I couldn't place my finger on, and you know I'm sorry I didn't listen to it sooner and didn't end things before they became so unlawful and toxic, I would have saved myself a lot of hurt if I had. You lead me to the place I am today, to become this person, to take this path and I thank you for that because I am truly happy. Happier than I thought I could be, for so many reasons: too many to write, too many to voice, too many to think of.

This is me acknowledging you, all the things you've done and all the things you continue to do.

This is me saying goodbye and
Thank you.

I have no words left to write about you, no words.
This page is being left
blank.

This is me saying goodbye to you
This is the start of something new.

VIII. Warm

One day you'll wake up, you will finally wake up and the sunlight will be streaming through the window in your room because you forgot to close the blinds the night before because your mind was filled with far more important things, like how your friends bought you all donuts and your hair dipped into the glaze and that you were surrounded by laughter, and your little brother, he's growing up and you are just in awe at how fast time moves and how proud you are to be in such a beautiful family with a mum who always dances to Billie Jean and a dog who wakes up every time eager for a new day with no worries or concerns, no thought of the day before and suddenly it dawns on you, with the suns warm rays on your face, that you haven't thought of him for months, he takes no place in your life anymore and that's the way it should have been a long time ago but today, today the day has finally come, and your body has fully released him, any minute particles that you were still holding on to have been let go, they have been thrown up into the very sun that has slowly warmed your heart since he left and it has finally done its job. You are fully thawed, you smile to yourself, you are warm.

The hole that you left in me has finally been filled.
I patched it back up and poured in what should have been there a long time ago.
I filled the hole with my own love, my own worth, my own value.
It has been filled with myself.

You make your own warmth darling
You make it all on your own.

And even in this cool, cool, air on a crisp clear night I feel warm because I am surrounded by those I love and we are laughing about all the old and new memories in this beautiful valley surrounded by mountains and looked down on by stars and they are speaking to my soul. I can hear the whispers of love as the winds brush past my ears and the leaves dip themselves into these honeyed rivers echoing the warmth that rushes through me, though all of us.

I have the best family I could have ever asked for, a mother who is stronger than she realises, the roots to my flowers, the strength in my bones. I have people who are always there for me, at the end of the phone, some at the end of the road, and this road of happiness will never end because I have found myself and those that fill my heart with love. I'm happy again, my work is done.

Surround yourself with people you love and know;
There's no better thing than feeling at home.

There's nothing better than returning to a warm enveloping hug.

(Mum, I feel safest in your arms)

Just because they don't contact you every day doesn't mean they have forgotten you. You will still be in their thoughts.

(Family, blood or not are forever.)

Sometimes all it takes is a talk with the people who water your roots and tend to your leaves in order for you to keep standing.

Sometimes you just find these people who make your life a little bit brighter. They are the sun in the darkest of winter days and the ones who make all the shit you go through worth it because they are always there at the end of it all.

It's these half drunken nights, talking about our shitty flatmates and how one day in the future we will find the true love we deserve, that I wouldn't change for anything.

Surround yourself with the good people, those you can be sat in a bar with, laughing and laughing and laughing because there is so much light and goodness in everyone's souls.

It's surprised me just how many good people have entered my life all of a sudden, but I honestly couldn't be more grateful.

And suddenly you wake up with a beaming smile on your face because last night you were surrounded by laughter and good people you had not met before and who you never expected to share such smiles with.

I want these memories to last forever.

I am happy,

I am

warm.

We caught eyes from across the room. The giddiness rose in me. I am okay again, I am ready for the warmth of something new.

Every time I read this, I fall in love with this little project of mine more and more. The poems still make me feel, they still get me through life and my struggles and the whirlwind of emotions that sometimes I face. I hope they can resonate with you too.

So, to all of you who were kind enough to buy this, read it, borrow it, look at it, connect with it, smile at it, cry over it, relate to it, inspire it, affect me in some way and cause me to write it,

I am eternally grateful,

Thank

You.

About the Author:

Cassie Senn, also known as @poems.c.h.s on Instagram, has been writing poetry for as long as she can remember. It all started in a blue notebook a very close family member gave her and slowly but surely, she filled the pages. Poetry is a way for her to deal with her emotions, feelings and thoughts as she progresses through life, transitioning from a teen to a young adult. Now 21, she decided this was the best time to do something with this project that she has been working on for many years. The book explores her own personal stories and events which she has endured, as well as conveying the stories of others in the hopes she can make people feel a little less alone in this great big world.

Printed in Great Britain
by Amazon

64417951R00121